TODAY'S
SUPERSTARS
Sports

Peyton
MANNING

by Geoffrey M. Horn

GARETH**STEVENS**
GS
P U B L I S H I N G
A Member of the WRC Media Family of Companies

Please visit our web site at: www.garethstevens.com
For a free color catalog describing Gareth Stevens Publishing's
list of high-quality books and multimedia programs, call
1-800-542-2595 (USA) or 1-800-387-3178 (Canada).

Library of Congress Cataloging-in-Publication Data

Horn, Geoffrey M.
    Peyton Manning / by Geoffrey M. Horn.
        p. cm. — (Today's superstars: sports)
    Includes bibliographical references and index.
    ISBN-13: 978-0-8368-6183-9 (lib. bdg.)
    ISBN-10: 0-8368-6183-3 (lib. bdg.)
    1. Manning, Peyton—Juvenile literature. 2. Football players—
United States—Biography—Juvenile literature.   I. Title.
GV939.M289H67   2006
796.332092—dc22   2005032081

This North American edition first published in 2006 by
Gareth Stevens Publishing
A Weekly Reader Company
200 First Stamford Place
Stamford, CT 06912 USA

This edition copyright © 2006 by Gareth Stevens, Inc.

Editor: Jim Mezzanotte
Art direction and design: Tammy West
Picture research: Diane Laska-Swanke

Photo credits: Cover, © Paul Jasienski/Getty Images; pp. 5, 7, 9, 17,
19, 23 © AP/Wide World Photos; p. 10 © Joe Robbins/Getty Images;
pp. 13, 24 © Al Messerschmidt/WireImage.com; p. 14 © George Long/
LPI/WireImage.com; p. 15 © Scott Burton/WireImage.com; p. 27
© Elsa/Getty Images

Printed in the United States of America

1 2 3 4 5 6 7 8 9 10 09 08 07

CONTENTS

CHAPTER 1

BREAKING THE RECORD

Peyton Manning has thrown more than four thousand passes in his pro career. But the touchdown (TD) pass he threw in his last home game of 2004 was something special.

It was the forty-ninth of the season, and it broke a record set by Dan Marino in 1984. Marino was one of the top quarterbacks (QBs) in pro football history. He was also one of Peyton's boyhood heroes.

Gunning for Number 49

For weeks, the National Football League (NFL) had been buzzing about Manning's

FACT FILE

Manning is big, strong, and quick. He stands 6 feet 5 inches (2 meters) tall and weighs 230 pounds (104 kilograms). He started every game in his first seven pro seasons.

Marino and Manning

One of Peyton Manning's favorite photos was taken when he was ten years old. It shows him with Dan Marino, who played quarterback for the Miami Dolphins for seventeen years. Marino still holds career records for passing attempts (8,358), completions (4,967), and touchdowns (420). He also holds the career record for passing yardage. Marino passed for a total of 61,361 yards, which adds up to almost 35 miles (56 kilometers)!

Marino joined the Dolphins in 1983 and was Rookie of the Year. He was voted Most Valuable Player (MVP) in 1984. He threw for forty-eight TDs that year. He also led the league with 362 completed passes in 564 attempts. He set a single-season passing record of 5,084 yards. Marino entered the Pro Football Hall of Fame in 2005.

Peyton pumps his fist after throwing the pass that shattered Marino's single-season touchdown record.

touchdown totals. He came into the game one TD short of Marino's record. On Sunday, December 26, more than 57,000 fans jammed the RCA Dome in Indianapolis. They hoped to see Peyton break the record at home.

It wasn't going to be easy. The Colts were hosting the San Diego Chargers. Each team was division champion. The Colts had taken the AFC South for the second straight year. The Chargers had won the AFC West for the first time since 1994.

The Chargers came out strong. They pressured Manning, sacking him four times. Peyton also fumbled twice and gave up an interception. "We might have been pressing a little bit to get those scoring passes," the Colts' coach, Tony Dungy, later said. "That goes for everyone on our team. Not just Peyton."

FACT FILE

A 2005 poll asked Americans to name their favorite sports stars. Among active players, Peyton Manning ranked first. He was followed by Tiger Woods, Brett Favre, and Derek Jeter.

Deep in the third quarter, Peyton threw a short pass to fullback James Mungro for a touchdown. Manning was now tied with Marino at forty-eight TDs. But the Chargers struck back. By the fourth quarter, they held a 31-16 lead. The Colts' Dominic Rhodes made the score 31-23 with an 88-yard runback of a kickoff.

Changing the Game Plan

Now it was time for Manning to make miracles. With about three minutes left in the game, the Colts had a third down on their own 15-yard line. They needed 15 yards for a first down. Peyton dropped back to pass, but the Chargers were all over him.

Colts fans cheer Peyton's record-breaking TD toss.

Somehow, he spotted running back Edgerrin James. James caught the ball in a crowd of defensive players.

With fourth down and 4 yards to go, the punting unit ran on the field. Frantically, Peyton waved them off. Instead, he threw to wide receiver Reggie Wayne for a 19-yard gain. The play gave the Colts a first down. It also gave Peyton a key piece of information. On the play, Colts wide receiver Brandon Stokley had run an outside pattern. The Chargers defender had put himself between Stokley and the sideline. What would happen, Peyton wondered, if Stokley faked outside but then headed toward the goalpost? Would the defender go for the fake?

With a minute to go in the game, Manning got his answer. He pretended to call the same play as before. Peyton put the ball in the air a full two seconds before

FACT FILE

Last-minute heroics during a game are nothing new to Manning. During his first seven years as a pro, he put together twenty-two game-winning drives in the fourth quarter or overtime. In each case, the Colts either came from behind or broke a tie to get the win.

Nick of Time

Peyton's parents, Archie and Olivia Manning, planned to be at the RCA Dome to see their son break Marino's record. But they almost missed Peyton's big moment. On Saturday, the day before the game, their flight from New Orleans to Indianapolis was canceled. They got on another plane on Sunday morning, but it took off late. At midday, the Mannings were stranded in Memphis, Tennessee. They were sure they had no way to get to the game in time to see Peyton play.

Finally, Colts owner Jim Irsay came to their rescue. He sent his own private plane to Memphis to pick them up. Peyton's parents got to the stadium with about eight minutes left in the game. They arrived just in time to see their son make football history.

Peyton's father, Archie Manning, almost missed his son's big day.

Stokley made his final break to the goalpost. The defender went for the fake. Then, he fell when he tried to recover.

Stokley was wide open in the end zone. "The ball was on me so quick, I'm just glad I was able to get my hands up," he told reporters. "I didn't have time to think about it." The catch gave Manning his record-breaking TD. It also gave the Colts a chance to tie the ball game. They went on to win in overtime, 34-31.

Later, Manning admitted the play hadn't been part of the Colts' game plan. They had never used it in a game before and only ran it twice in practice. "You think the NFL is real complex," he said. "But it turns into street ball real quick."

The Colts' thrilling overtime win against the Chargers gave Peyton and his fans a lot to celebrate.

ARCHIE'S KIDS

CHAPTER 2

Peyton Williams
Manning was
born in New Orleans,
Louisiana, on March 24,
1976. He grew up in a
football family. His
father, Archie, was
starting quarterback for
the New Orleans Saints.

College Sweethearts

Archie was born in 1949. He attended
high school in Drew, Mississippi. In
1971, he married his college sweetheart,
Olivia Williams.

Olivia was in high school in Philadelphia,
Mississippi, when she first saw Archie. She
was at a basketball game, watching her
school's team lose to his. "That night we
got upset by this little Drew team," she recalls.
"There was Archie, as cocky-looking a player
as I'd ever seen. Long red hair. Tall and
skinny. Dribbling the ball behind his back. ...
Making shots from every angle."

The two met again when both were students at the University of Mississippi, or "Ole Miss." Archie was impressed. In *Manning*, a book he wrote with Peyton, he recalls: "She was pretty. She was tall and willowy, like a model. She was vivacious. She was smart. And she knew football." They began dating and soon fell in love. By their senior year at Ole Miss, Archie was a star QB and Olivia was Homecoming Queen.

Football at an Early Age
Peyton's older brother Cooper was born in March 1974. Cooper was five and Peyton three when the two boys started playing football games in the Mannings' backyard. Was it touch football? No way, says Peyton. They played tackle, with full uniforms, pads, and helmets. The boys even had lockers in their rooms. Peyton says they would start each game by singing the

FACT FILE

Hurricane Katrina destroyed much of New Orleans in late August 2005. Fortunately, the Manning home suffered little damage. Peyton and his younger brother Eli helped send thousands of pounds of supplies to hurricane victims. Eli plays QB for the New York Giants.

First Date

In *Manning*, Archie tells the story of his first date with Olivia. Before the date, Olivia phoned her father.

"Hey, daddy, guess who I'm going out with tonight?"

"Who?"

"Remember that show-off from Drew who beat us in basketball?"

"Archie Manning?"

"Yes. It looks like he might be Ole Miss's next varsity quarterback."

Her daddy was pleased. He said, "When are you gonna bring him home for dinner so we can approve of him?"

This 1998 photo shows Peyton with his mother, Olivia Manning.

Archie's Quarterback Career

Archie Manning was one of the greatest college players ever. People at Ole Miss still talk about the game he had against Alabama in 1969. 'Bama won, 33-32. But Archie put on a show, passing for 436 yards and running for 104. The game, on national TV, made him one of the country's best-known college players. "That game was the most fun I ever had," says Archie.

Archie spent most of his pro career with the New Orleans Saints. The Saints had high hopes when they made him their number-one pick in 1971. But the team never had a winning season the whole time he was there. The best they could do was an 8-8 record in 1979. Sometimes they were so bad that people called them the Ain'ts instead of the Saints.

As QB for the New Orleans Saints, Archie Manning was a very good player on a very bad team.

The Mannings — Peyton, Cooper, Eli, and Archie — gathered at Ole Miss in October 2003 for a game against Alabama. As QB, Eli led the Ole Miss team to a 43-28 victory.

National Anthem — or as many words of it as the boys could remember.

Because their father was the Saints' QB, Peyton and Cooper had special privileges. They were allowed to watch the team practice on Saturday mornings. They could come into the locker room after the game. But Archie and Olivia never pushed their sons to become athletes. "They always just encouraged us to play sports and just to enjoy it," Peyton recalls. "It was never a pressure situation. I think that's still today why I have such a love for the game — why I still have so much fun playing football."

SCHOOL DAYS

The Manning boys went to Isidore Newman, a private school in New Orleans. By seventh grade, Peyton was playing on the school's football team, the Greenies. He always played quarterback. He never wanted to be on defense or special teams. If anyone asked him what position he wanted aside from QB, he would say, "Coach."

Peyton, Cooper, and the Greenies

In tenth grade, Peyton became the starting QB. Cooper, a senior, was a wide receiver. On the field, the brothers used hand signals and code words that only they knew.

FACT FILE

In college, Cooper was told he had to quit football. Doctors found that he had a serious problem with his spine. Cooper had always worn number 18. After Cooper stopped playing, Peyton started wearing 18 as a tribute to his brother.

Learning by Watching

When Peyton was in high school, he began studying NFL game films. "If you're going to watch film, do it the right way," his father told him. Archie meant that when you watch a quarterback make a big play, you shouldn't just watch the ball. You need to study what the defenders did, and how the offense beat them.

In high school and college, advice from Archie helped Peyton sharpen his quarterback skills.

Peyton remembers completing about 110 passes that season. Almost 80 of them went to his brother. Cooper gained 1,250 yards and was the Greenies' MVP.

By his senior year, Peyton had become one of the nation's top high school players. In three years with the Greenies, he passed for 7,207 yards and ninety-two TDs. Of the thirty-nine games he started, the team won thirty-four. After his final season, he was named Gatorade Circle of Champions National Player of the Year.

Tough Choices

In early 1994, Peyton faced a tough choice. His father and mother had gone to the University of Mississippi. Cooper had gone there, too. Years later, Peyton's other brother, Eli, would also choose Ole Miss.

But Peyton wasn't sure if Ole Miss was the right place for him. "Being Archie

FACT FILE

Peyton was a freshman at the University of Tennessee when he met Ashley Thompson. She was a student at the University of Virginia. Without any public fanfare, the couple got engaged during the summer of 2000. They were married on March 17, 2001.

Life Skills

Peyton Manning is a great quarterback. But there's a lot he doesn't know. Just ask one of his childhood friends, Walker Jones. He says Peyton can tell you every coverage any defense has used against him. "But if you ask him to turn a lawn mower on, or scramble some eggs — anything as basic as that, he doesn't have a clue how to do it." Peyton's brother Eli agrees: "I don't know if he knows how to work a washing machine or not. He has no sense of direction. . . . He's always having to call people."

Some of his teammates joke about Peyton's fashion choices. "We give him a hard time," says wide receiver Brandon Stokley. "You know, he usually wears tight jeans and cowboy boots. You know, it seems like the guy's making so much money. . . . He could find somebody to help him dress!"

At the University of Tennessee, Peyton excelled at passing the ball and picking apart opponents' defenses.

Manning's son, no matter where I go, there'll be pressure," he said. "Being the son of a former quarterback, they expect you to do well. Going to Ole Miss will be more pressure because that's where my dad made his name."

After weeks of agonizing, Peyton announced his decision — and shocked Ole Miss fans. He had chosen a rival school, the University of Tennessee (UT).

At UT, Peyton shined both on and off the field. In four years there, he started forty-five games. The Volunteers won thirty-nine of them. He broke records with 863 pass completions for 11,201 yards. Incredibly, opponents intercepted only 33 of his 1,381 pass attempts. He also earned excellent grades.

Peyton faced another tough choice at the end of his junior year. He'd finished his course work. He could have left UT and joined the NFL. But something told him he needed another year in school. "My college experience was a really good one," he says. "I knew I had a chance to slow things down a little bit. . . . I just wanted to enjoy being a college senior."

LEARNING HIS CRAFT

As a senior, Peyton had a great season. He passed for 3,819 yards and thirty-six touchdowns. The Vols won eleven of thirteen games and the Southeastern Conference title.

The only down note was a 42-17 loss to Nebraska in the Orange Bowl. Playing with a bad knee, Manning completed twenty-one of thirty-one passes, but for only 134 yards. The Vols also had three turnovers in the first half. "That killed us," said Peyton. "You can't turn over the ball against a great team like Nebraska and expect to win."

FACT FILE

In 1997, Peyton won the Sullivan Award as the top U.S. amateur athlete. Both Peyton and his brother Eli won the Maxwell Award as College Player of the Year. Peyton won it in 1997. Eli won in 2003.

Growing Pains

When NFL teams chose new players in 1998, Manning was the top pick. He was taken by the Indianapolis Colts. His six-year contract included a signing bonus of $11.6 million. The Colts had a 3-13 record in 1997. They needed a jolt, and fans needed a new hero.

Peyton's first regular-season game, against the Miami Dolphins, showed how good he could be. It also showed how much he still had to learn. He completed twenty-one of thirty-seven passes for 302 yards. But he also threw three interceptions and was sacked four times. With Dan Marino at QB, the Dolphins won, 24-15.

During Peyton's rookie year, the Colts had their second straight 3-13 season. He passed for twenty-six TDs. But he also threw twenty-eight interceptions. Before the NFL, he had always been on winning teams. Now he would have to live with — and

FACT FILE

The Colts played in Baltimore for three decades before moving to Indianapolis in 1984. The top QB for the Baltimore Colts was Johnny Unitas. He led the team to NFL championships in 1958 and 1959.

The One Hundred Club

The NFL has a special way to rate quarterbacks. The system uses five numbers: (1) attempted passes; (2) completed passes; (3) passing yardage; (4) touchdown passes; (5) interceptions. The formula is complicated, but the meaning is simple. A quarterback who has a rating of 100 or higher is having a fantastic season.

Peyton had a rating of 71.2 in his first year, which is good for a rookie. But since then, his improvement has been spectacular. In 2004, he hit 121.1 — the highest rating in the history of the NFL. During the regular season, he completed 336 passes in 497 attempts. He passed for 4,557 yards and a record-breaking forty-nine TDs. Peyton's rating was also over 100 in 2005 and 2006.

Manning holds up a team jersey after the Colts made him their top pick in 1998. Joining him are Colts owner Jim Irsay (left) and NFL chief Paul Tagliabue.

learn from — losing. "You don't really accept it," he said. "You just deal with it."

Turnaround

Colts fans didn't have to wait very long for things to get better. In 1999, the team went 13-3, the greatest one-year turnaround in NFL history. Manning cut his interceptions to fifteen. He also had his first 400-yard game. With Peyton calling the plays, Marvin Harrison became one of the league's most feared receivers. Edgerrin James rushed for 1,553 yards and was Rookie of the Year.

Defensive problems held the Colts back the next several years. Peyton was uneven. He'd be brilliant one game, flawed the next. The Colts made the play-offs in 1999, 2000,

Peyton's rookie season showed he still had a lot to learn.

and 2002. But the team lost in the first round each time.

Another big breakthrough came in 2003. The Colts had a regular-season record of 12-4. Peyton ranked first in the NFL in completions (379) and passing yardage (4,267). He shared Most Valuable Player (MVP) honors with QB Steve McNair of the Tennessee Titans.

Almost Perfect

In the play-offs, the Colts first destroyed the Denver Broncos, 41-10. Then, they outgunned the Kansas City Chiefs, 38-31. In these two wins, Peyton threw for eight TDs. Not one of his passes was intercepted. For two weeks in a row, the Colts never had to punt.

The AFC title game was next. Only the New England Patriots stood between the Colts and the Super Bowl. Against the Broncos and the Chiefs, Peyton had been near-perfect. Could he make it three in a row against the Pats' defense? The answer was no. The Pats picked off four of Peyton's passes, and the Colts lost, 24-14.

Manning made no excuses. "I just made some bad throws, some bad decisions," he told reporters after the game. "I thought the Patriots played extremely well, and we didn't."

CHAPTER 5

THE GREATEST QUARTERBACK EVER?

For the Colts, 2004 looked like a replay of 2003. Once again, the Colts faced the Patriots in the play-offs, and once again, the Pats shut down Peyton's passing attack. Led by QB Tom Brady, the Pats humbled the Colts, 20-3. They went on to win their third Super Bowl in four years. Still, Colts fans had a lot to cheer about. Manning had another MVP year. His three favorite wide receivers — Marvin Harrison, Brandon Stokley, and Reggie Wayne — also made history. Each caught passes for more

FACT FILE

Playing the St. Louis Rams in October 2005, Manning and Marvin Harrison teamed up for a record eighty-sixth TD pass. Steve Young and Jerry Rice held the previous record of eighty-five.

The PeyBack Bowl

In 1999, Peyton Manning set up the PeyBack Foundation. This agency helps kids in need. It has given more than $1 million to youth groups in Indiana, Tennessee, and Louisiana. In August 2005, the "PeyBack Bowl" — a bowling event — raised more than $260,000 to help poor children in Indianapolis.

With three touchdown passes, Peyton was MVP of the all-star Pro Bowl game in February 2005.

than 1,000 yards and at least ten TDs. It was the first time three receivers on the same team had done so in a single season.

Getting Better

Manning has set new standards for a pro quarterback. He is the only QB in NFL history to pass for at least 3,000 yards in each of his first nine seasons. For six years in a row, from 1999 to 2004, he threw for at least 4,000 yards, another NFL record. He's also the only QB in NFL history to pass for at least twenty-five TDs in nine straight seasons.

In 2006, Peyton and the Colts had another outstanding season, plowing through the play-offs and reaching Super Bowl XLI. On February 4, 2007, Peyton led his team to its first Super Bowl victory since 1971.

FACT FILE

Peyton is one of the NFLs highest-paid players. In March 2004, he signed a seven-year contract worth $98 million. The deal included a $34.5 million signing bonus.

TIME LINE

1976	Peyton Williams Manning is born March 24 in New Orleans, Louisiana
1993	As a high school senior, Manning is named Gatorade Circle of Champions National Player of the Year.
1994	Decides to attend the University of Tennessee instead of Ole Miss.
1997	Wins the Sullivan Award as the top U.S. amateur athlete and the Maxwell Award as College Player of the Year.
1998	As the number-one NFL pick, Manning is chosen by the Indianapolis Colts.
2003	Shares the regular-season MVP award with Titans QB Steve McNair.
2004	Signs a seven-year, $98-million contract with the Colts. He throws a record forty-nine TD passes and is named MVP for the second year in a row.
2005	Manning and wide receiver Marvin Harrison set a new record for TD passes.
2007	The Colts defeat the Chicago Bears in Super Bowl XLI. Manning is the MVP.

GLOSSARY

AFC — short for the American Football Conference, a grouping of teams in the NFL. Each season, the winners of the AFC and the NFC (National Football Conference) compete in the Super Bowl for the NFL championship.

amateur — someone who competes in a sport without being paid for it.

defense — in football, the group of players who try to stop the opposing team from scoring.

first down — the first of four attempts that a team gets to move the football down the field. If a team moves the ball a certain distance, it gets another first down and can run four more plays.

offense — in football, the group of players who try to move the ball down the field to score.

quarterback (QB) — the player who directs the offense and usually passes the ball.

sacked — for quarterbacks, tackled behind the line where the offense and defense meet, usually while trying to pass.

turnover — the loss of the ball by the offense, either through a fumble or an interception of a pass.

wide receiver — a player on offense whose main job is traveling down the field to catch a pass.

TO FIND OUT MORE

BOOKS

Peyton Manning. Amazing Athletes (series). Jeff Savage (LernerSports)

Peyton Manning. Benchmark All-Stars (series). Michael Bradley (Marshall Cavendish)

Peyton Manning. Sports Great Books (series). Barry Wilner (Enslow Publishers)

VIDEOS

The Story of the 2003 Indianapolis Colts: Heart of a Champion (Warner Home Video) NR

WEB SITES

Indianapolis Colts
www.colts.com
Colts' official site. Includes news and photos, plus audio and video highlights

NFL.com
www.nfl.com/
Official site of the National Football League

Peyton Manning
http://peytonmanning.com/
Peyton's official web site

INDEX

About the Author

Geoffrey M. Horn has been a fan of music, movies, and sports for as long as he can remember. He has written more than two dozen books for young people and adults, along with hundreds of articles for encyclopedias and other works. He lives in southwestern Virginia, in the foothills of the Blue Ridge Mountains, with his wife, their collie, and four cats. He dedicates this book to the people of New Orleans.